minimalist interiors

minimalist interiors

COLLINS|DESIGN

An Imprint of HarperCollins*Publishers*

MINIMALIST INTERIORS
Copyright © 2005 by HARPER DESIGN and LOFT Publications

First published in 2005 by:
Harper Design,
An Imprint of HarperCollins*Publishers*
10 East 53rd Street
New York, NY 10022
Tel.: (212) 207-7000
Fax: (212) 207-7654
HarperDesign@harpercollins.com
www.harpercollins.com

Distributed throughout the world by:
HarperCollins International
10 East 53rd Street
New York, NY 10022
Fax: (212) 207-7654

HarperCollins books may be purchased for educational, business, or sales promotional use.
For information, please write: Special Markets Department, HarperCollins Publishers Inc.,
10 East 53rd Street, New York, NY 10022

Publisher:
Paco Asensio

Editorial coordination:
Quim Rosell

Translation:
Richard L. Rees

Art Director:
Mireia Casanovas Soley

Graphic Design and Layout:
Diego González

Library of Congress Cataloging-in-Publication Data

Rosell, Quim
  Minimalist Interiors / Quim Rosell.
    p. cm.
  Includes index.
  ISBN 0-06-082990-7 (paperback)
  1. Minimal architecture. 2. Interior architecture. 3. Architecture, Domestic. I. Title
  NA682.M55R67 2005
  728--dc22

                    2005001307

Printed by: Anman Gràfiques del Vallès
Spain
D.L: B-4820-05

Second Printing, 2005

Contents

Both in theory and practice, recent 1990s architecture may be placed in a broad context that does not lend itself to precise definition. Even so, it has reserved a place for one of the trends that has been applied progressively as a response to over abundance in design and to excessive deconstructivist formalism: Minimalism. When confronted with the term "minimalist architecture," we are bound to turn to Minimal Art, a contemporary artistic movement that emerged in North America in the 1960s as a critical response to the artistic climate created by other movements of the time such as abstract Expressionism, Pop Art, and Op Art.

Thus, a diversified artistic output, combined with an accumulation of radical, challenging research and experimentation, emerged with the purpose of obtaining maximum tension with minimal means. Indeed, minimal art seeks the essential through the use of simple, elementary geometrical structures as a formal vehicle, and through the absence of decorative elements. In this way, all allusions or references are excluded, except for the repetition of forms as a physical presence in a specific place—a clear allusion to the process of industrial production—or the choice of material (either conventional or industrial) in order to establish relationships with the location, the site, the mass, the surroundings, and so on. In general terms, minimalism is based on a reduction of architecture down to its essential concepts of space, light and form, rather than on mechanisms of subtraction, negation, or absence of ornament. Even so, a superficial reading might lead to the mistaken idea of predetermined

appearances or a series of conventions (such as white monochrome or the cult of the void), which would enormously oversimplify the complexity of the term minimalism and give way to its introduction into any cultural context. Unlike Minimal Art—with its critical sights aimed at preestablished concepts—minimalist architecture, which lacks any kind of social ideology, is an appendix or continuation of some aspects of contemporary architecture, emerging as a widely used tool in current architectural practice. It provides examples on the one hand of stringent sophistication in the finishes of materials, and of technical cleanliness on the other. Minimalism also sets up an intense dialogue with the site and its surroundings to the extent of transforming them and endowing them with a new identity, and seeks unity through repetition as a guarantee of quality.

The Hakuei house
Akira Sakamoto

Photos © Nacása and Partners

Osaka, Japan

The site is flanked by two streets, one of which forms a "T" intersection with a third. These characteristics were taken into account when it came to designing the house. Across the site, views flow east-west from one street to the other. The eye of the passerby may look freely through the building from the intersection of the streets toward a small wood on the other side. In this way, the volume of the house becomes light and permeable to the eye.

The basic design concept was to represent the exterior in the interior and the interior in the exterior, thereby creating a continuous space between the two. The space is articulated by discontinuous walls, in which the openings produce a sensation of fluidity and continuity. People can look and talk through the patio and the deck. Glimpses of the occupants can be seen behind the walls, establishing links between interior and exterior spaces. Each room differs from the others by the way it is entered, in its visual relationships, and in the way it is lit, which may be through a skylight, horizontal windows, or narrow slits in the corners.

The house was designed on the basic precepts of minimalist art: the dramatic treatment of the light; the noble materials; the simple forms; and the position of elements in relation to others.

The cladding of the walls that constitute the patio is the same as that of the interior, which reinforces the relationship and continuity between interior and exterior. The tree is the only element in the patio, and represents the synthesis of the cycles of nature, living beings, and time.

This architecture propitiates silence and reflection, and directs gazes and thought toward minimal things that elsewhere would be smothered by noise.

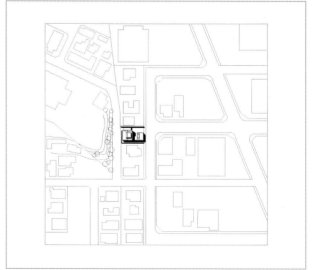

Japanese architecture centers its attention on details that constitute the essence of elements.

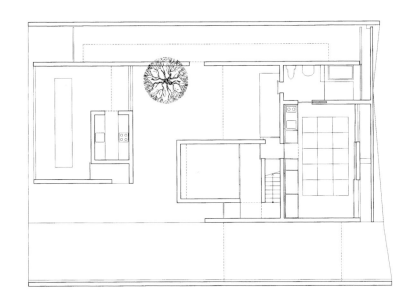

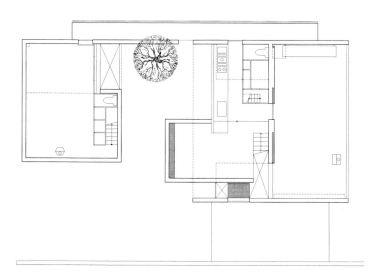

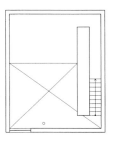

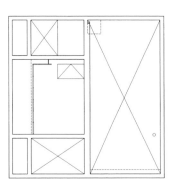

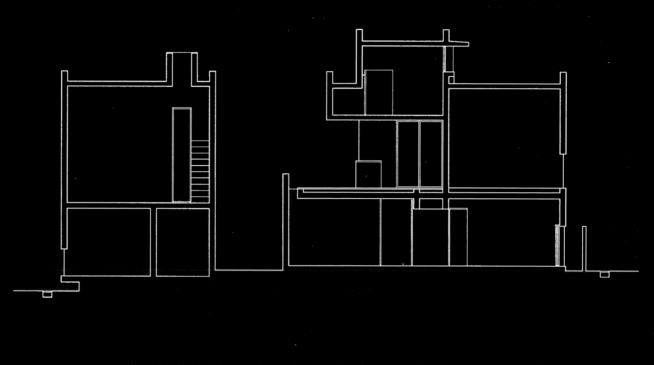

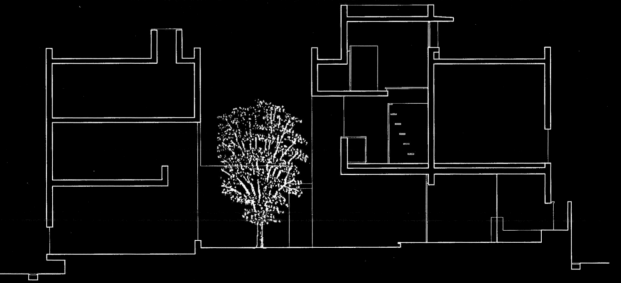

The Moerkerke house
John Pawson

Photos © Richard Glover

London, UK

In this project, a traditional Victorian mews was converted into a home for three people. To take better advantage of the limited space available, the kitchen, bathroom and stairs were relocated. The bottom floor, which accommodates the kitchen, living room, and dining room, was left as open as possible to create a large continuous space that can be subdivided in the future if necessary.

Two further elements were added to modify the proportions of the interior space and to meet the functional needs of the dwelling: a chimney wall that contains a staircase, and a wall that both defines and conceals the kitchen. The staircase, which squeezes tightly into the chimney wall, is generously lit from the skylight above. The kitchen features a stainless steel canopy over the cooker. The flooring both upstairs and downstairs is of cherry wood, and the walls, all painted white, create a calm atmosphere that fosters reflection. The windows are covered with white fabric that filters the light and visually isolates the home from the outside. A simple table replete with six chairs by Wegner and two pairs of armchairs by Christian Liagre are the only visible pieces of furniture.

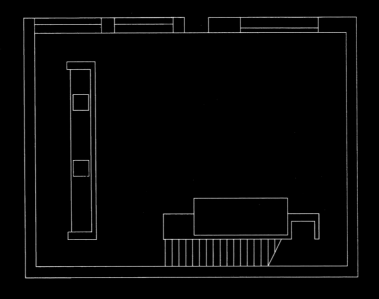

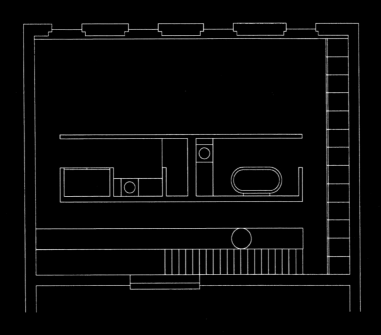

The vertical partitions are designed to appear subtle and light, and are separated by a gap from both the floor and the ceiling.

This project involved the renovation of an old traditional Mallorcan house in the island's interior. The facade, together with the two adjacent utility buildings (the janitor's house and the owner's office), have all been preserved, while a sober and very contemporary atmosphere has been created inside.

A strong timber partition separates the house from the janitor's dwelling and delimits a large private patio. The architect also designed the garden, and sought to link it directly to the house through the pavement, a combination of concrete and local stone.

A washbasin created from a single large stone inserted into a niche attracts attention by virtue of its theatrical quality. The same atmosphere pervades the entire house. The furniture, stringently designed for each room, has a simple, bare, almost monastic quality. Materials such as wood, ceramic, and marble delicately combine to create an elegant and relaxing atmosphere. The entrance is a room whose walls, covered with timber panels, conceal the entry to the guest bathroom. From here, access is gained to the kitchen/dining room and to the stairway that leads to the floor above, which accommodates the bedrooms.

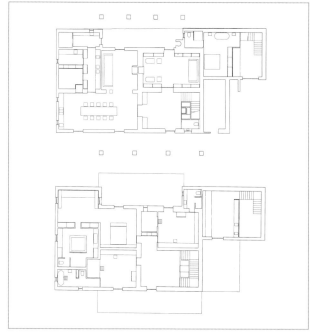

This house reveals that minimalism is a timeless concept, applicable even to architecture of the past.

A former fire station in the West End of London has been refurbished as the home of a couple: a musician and a chef. The building is long and narrow, and there were not enough windows to illuminate the whole interior with natural light. Therefore, the decision was made to build a metal and glass structure on the roof to flood the spaces below with natural light. This glazed ceiling can be opened in summer to convert the space into a pleasant terrace. The dividing screens on all three floors were eliminated, and a stone staircase was built against one of the side walls, which climbs from the ground-floor entrance to the greenhouse on the top floor. A large, wooden, arch-shaped structure acts as storage space and contains the stairs, separating them from the rest of the apartment. The second floor accommodates a vestibule, the master bedroom complete with bathroom, two small bedrooms, and an additional bathroom. On this floor the wooden structure contains a large collection of records and also serves as a writing desk.

Much of the furniture was designed by the architect and is built in. This is true for the bed in the master bedroom, of the bathtub, and the wooden structure that contains the stairs.

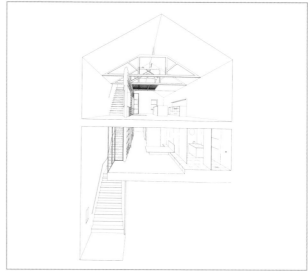

The architect's strategy was to create a solid relationship between space and the objects that occupy it. The best way to achieve this is to design both elements.

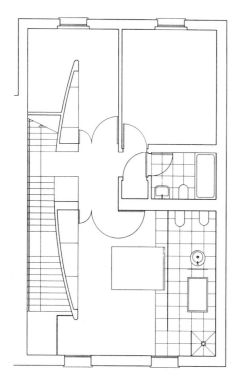

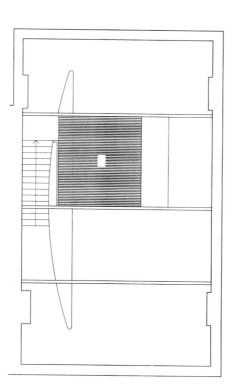

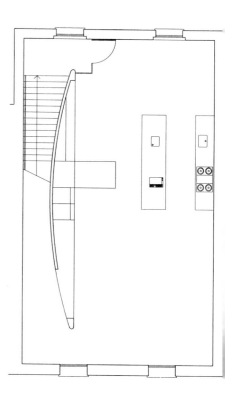

House in Vienna
Rataplan

Photos © Markus Tomaselli, Rataplan

Vienna, Austria

This building, constructed in 1901, was refurbished in 1992. Four duplex homes (between 430 and 1,620 square feet) and three apartments were built, which together account for 9,200 square feet of living space. Different design criteria were applied inside, since all seven owners participated actively in the process. Many of the homes are oriented to the south and look over the peaceful interior patio that, together with the garden, were raised half a story to accommodate a garage. On the ground floor there are two stores.

The street facade was left practically intact, unlike the rear facade, to which an annex-like structure was added. This structure was conceived as a conservatory for each of the homes. These conservatories need no heating, and in spring and fall they retain solar energy. In summer the entire facade may be closed behind metal shutters.

Two of the duplex homes have their stairways in the annex, which in turn is suspended from a hanging metal structure.

The window frames are made of aluminum and are quite large, to suggest the look of a terrace. The appearance of the facade may change according to the use the owners make of the metal window shutters. From the exterior, it is possible to subtly perceive the life going on inside the homes.

The original staircase was very dark, but now a narrow window running from bottom to top allows light to penetrate the building.

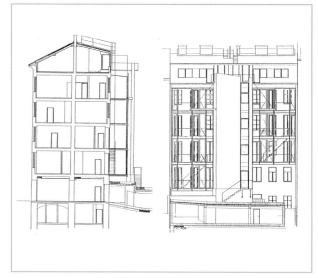

Some of the partitions are translucent, in order to allow natural light to penetrate.

The furniture is the product of an exclusive design that combines wood, glass and aluminum.

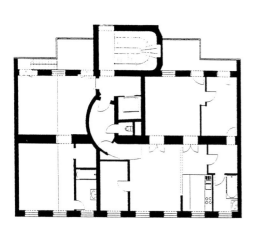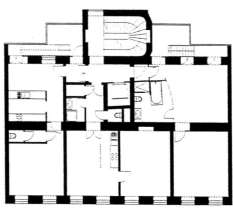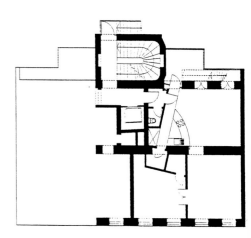

House in El Pedregal
Grupo LBC

Photos © Fernando Cordero

Mexico DF, Mexico

The house stands on a large site that slopes sharply down toward the street, from which it is separated by a sturdy existing wall of local volcanic stone. The house is arranged around a large central patio, the element that governs its composition as a whole.

Vehicle access is gained by means of a driveway that serves three other homes; the four together form a larger complex. This site determined the position of the garage and the service zone. From the longest edge of the site, parallel to the street and to the volcanic stone wall, a stone stair leads to the main entrance, which is framed by a strong steel girder contained between the wall and the solid service volume, also of stone.

The foyer is separated from the living area by a large fireplace. From here the interior opens with a diagonal view of the patio, which is framed by large oxidized steel porticoes. The pilasters are sturdy triangular prisms, the edges of which point towards this open space. Some of them are submerged in the water of a large pond that flows gently through the patio, cutting it diagonally.

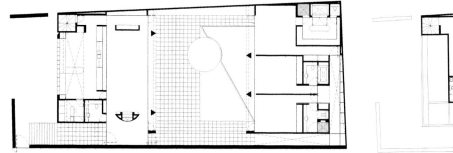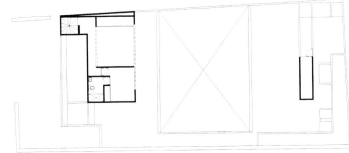

Coelho house
Andrade Morettin Arquitetos

Photos © Nelson Kon

São Paulo, Brazil

This house consists of two interconnected volumes, of which the structure and materials clearly contrast with each other. These two structures (a main space and a service space) are arranged along a longitudinal axis and take advantage of the shade provided by the trees.

The main body is a foyer of 31 by 13 ft consisting of a light jatobá timber framework structure surrounded by panels of alveolar polycarbonate. This translucent membrane gives way at one of its corners to a wall of glass that frames the view of a nearby lake. A curtain that can define a dark, more private environment establishes the limits of the bedroom area. The regular layout of the underground electrical installation completes the necessary infrastructure for this space.

Owing to both design and construction concerns, this "light box" stands above-ground on a support. The floating corrugated sheet-metal roof contributes to the effect of weightlessness.

The service structure is conceived as a rock that emerges from the ground in the form of wide ceramic walls that protect the main pavilion from the afternoon sun. It contains the kitchen, washroom, and bathroom. The benches in the kitchen and the bathroom, the cupboards, and the shower partitions are made of either in masonry or concrete. The position and dimensions of the few openings respond strictly to their function, thus emphasizing a heavy, fixed character that contrasts with the character of the translucent panels.

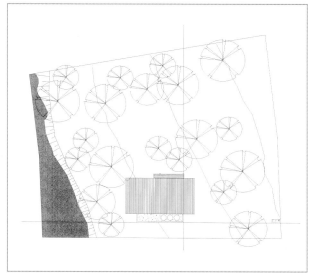

The different views of this architectural object respond to the different degrees of transparency of its skin.

The distorted perception of the polycarbonate panels place the house somewhere between abstraction and reality itself.

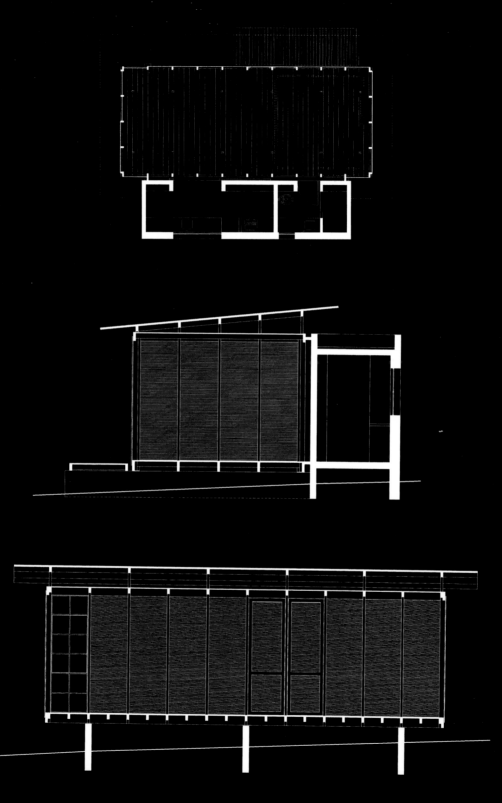

Sperl house
Adolf Krischanitz

Photos © Chris Pfaff, Margherita Spiluttini

Vienna, Austria

The construction of this house had to form part of a plan for the entire area that included a total of 150 dwellings arranged on long, narrow plots that formed larger complexes. The dimensions of each plot—25 ft wide by between 197 and 490 ft long—made it necessary to construct semi-detached houses of no more than two stories that still allowed natural light to penetrate the interiors, despite the strict building conditions. The resulting form follows the site's criteria but still takes advantage of modern-day technology and materials.

The general plan for the zone allowed for the creation of a large natural space in the middle of each plots, which by virtue of their dimensions was required to provide high density on relatively limited surface area. This was achieved through the use of the long patios characteristic of the area that make it possible to achieve simple linear subdivisions along the length of each plot.

Through the strict application of requirements, combined with the use of advanced technology, this architectural style was generated to construct semi-detached buildings of considerable length, thus forming a series of different units that may be extended according to the preferences and needs of each home owner. This construction technique joins two different elements: those of traditional construction with the requirements of the site.

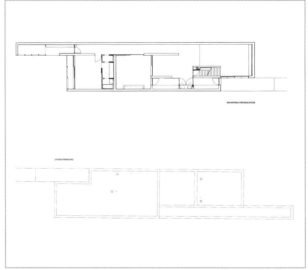

Concrete is a major presence, both on ceilings and on walls. The joins of the plank moulding have been preserved.

The architecture of this dwelling consists of an interplay between two-directional planes, some of which are structural, while others have a purely distributional function.

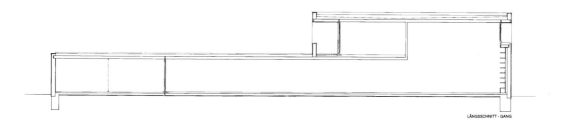

LÄNGSSCHNITT - GANG

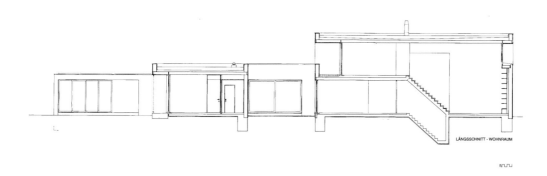

LÄNGSSCHNITT - WOHNRAUM

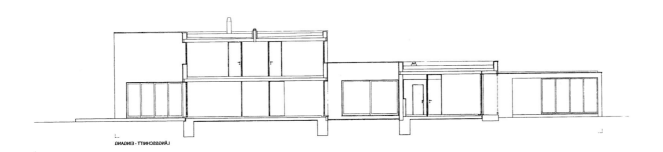

LÄNGSSCHNITT - EINGANG

Given the length of the plot and the narrowness of the facade, considerable effort was devoted to designing the means to allow natural light to penetrate.

Extension of a single-family house
Philippe Madec

Photos © Hervé Abbadie

Chambourcy, France

The alterations in this project consist basically of the extension of the original structure at ground level, which groups together the main entrance, the toilets, an office, a salon and a living room. All the floors of the old house have also been altered: the existing basement, difficult to access, has been converted into a storehouse and bathroom; the kitchen and dining room have been moved to the ground floor; the two existing bedrooms on the second floor were preserved in their original locations; and the attic now houses a study and an installations room. New windows have been added to some of the rooms, and the garden has been transformed into a extension of the interior.

The materials used for this renovation consist of a cladding for the interior vertical faces of the same color as the existing house, the facade overlooking the garden was glazed and framed by dark metal profiles, the exterior perimeter walls were faced in a gray-beige material that was extended into the home's interior, and both the chimney and the roof are made of zinc.

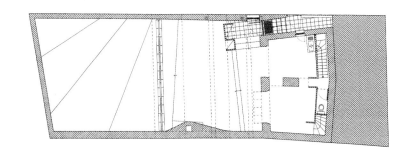

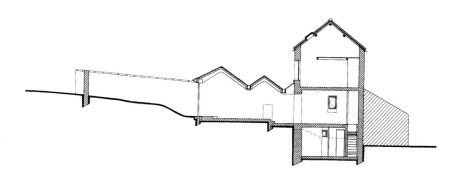

The wavy ceiling creates different visual effects depending on the light that penetrates the interior.

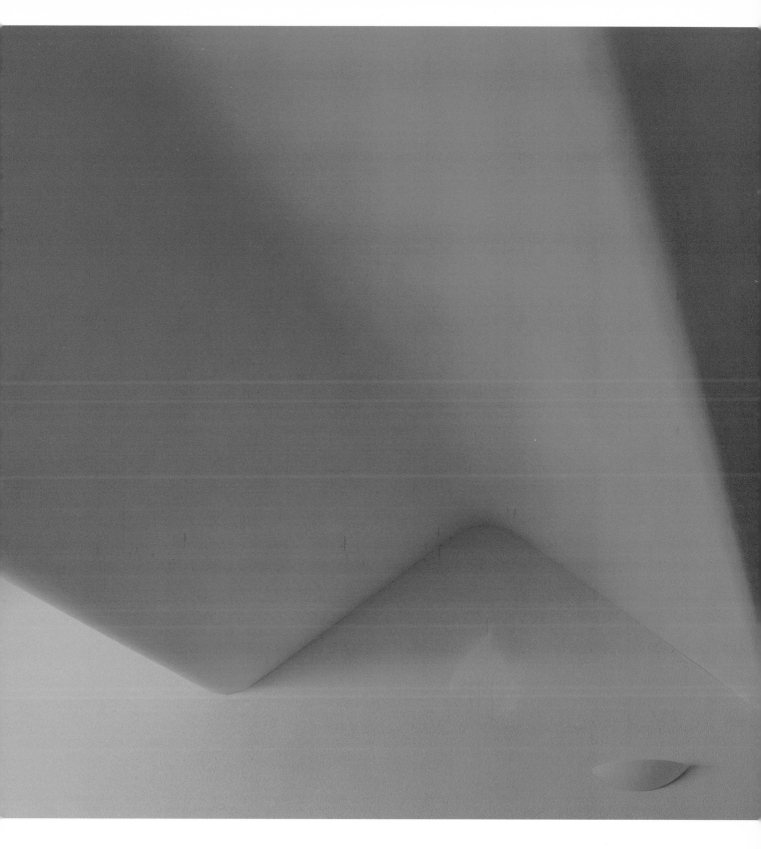

The H house
Sauerbruch Hutton Architects

Photos © Hélène Binet

London, UK

This project consists of the remodeling of a three-story house built in Kensington in 1967 by architect James Melvin. The new structure consists of a 32 by 32 ft concrete cube, an innovative spatial element that adds new vibrantly colored rooms to the original structure. Each floor presents a different ambience.

On the ground floor a large translucent glass pane separates the entrance from the swimming pool and garden behind. The interior spaces are separated from the exterior only by sliding glass panels. The second floor has an open plan, with broad windows offering panoramic views on two sides. The top floor—the bedrooms and guest apartment—create a world of privacy, sensuality and luxury.

In order to preserve spatial flexibility, the different zones are defined by brightly colored furniture—objects where utensils of everyday life are kept. The dialogue between these colored forms and the ubiquitous presence of the garden constitutes a dense and urban combination of nature and architecture.

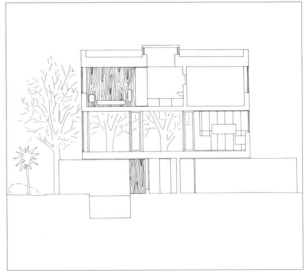

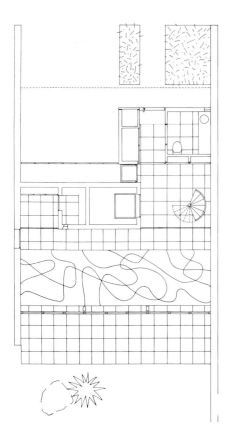

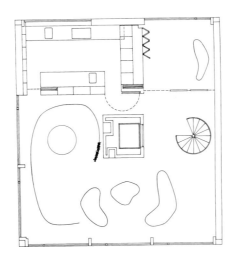

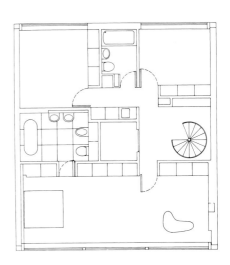

This project consisted of the renovation of an old two-story house standing on a site 25 ft wide by 246 ft long. The alterations took the form of large open spaces, two bedrooms, a study and a swimming pool looking north at the rear of the house.

The width of the site allowed the architect considerable flexibility when it came to designing the kitchen area, which lies on one of the sides. This left room for open, light-flooded spaces. The ground floor is divided by a plywood structure that separates the living/dining room from the kitchen. These spaces open onto the patio at the rear of the house, with a swimming pool along one of its sides. The threshold connecting the kitchen and the patio may be converted into an informal dining area, if so desired.

On the first floor, the same strategy of subdividing space was applied through the use of a wooden structure placed lengthwise, parallel to the stairs. It serves as a closet for both bedrooms and the changing room. The bathroom is located at the rear of the house and faces the swimming pool. The second-floor study opens onto a terrace with excellent views of the city and Harbour Bridge.

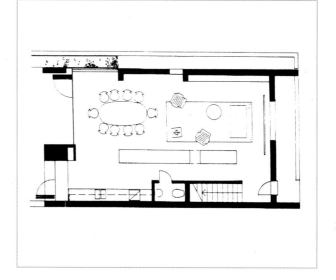

Ground floor

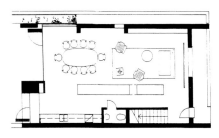

First floor

Second floor

The house without walls
Shigeru Ban

Photos © Hiroyuki Hirai

Nagano, Japan

This pavilion forms part of a series of experimental projects that the architect calls "Case Study Houses." Built on a steep slope, and designed to minimize excavation work, the rear half of this house has been inserted into the earth. The ground curves at one end to meet the roof slab, which rests only on three very slender poles. The fundamental concept behind this house is to establish spatial continuity both inside and outside. Two planes, defined by the floor and the roof, create and frame a horizon. Limits have been eliminated: the inner space has no partitions and even the bathroom is exposed to view. Only the kitchen unit, a bench, and a few pieces of furniture suggest zone differentiation in what is essentially a single, homogeneous space.

The interior is transformed by sliding panels, which allow many different possibilities and endow the room with a new character. The curvilinear forms are very simple, allowing their structure to almost disappear, and the transparency of the walls creates the impression that the house is a part of the landscape.

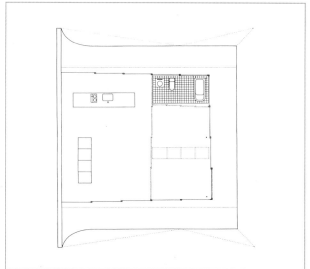

Although the concepts that govern the project defy functionality, they are theoretical achievements that serve as examples for other architects.

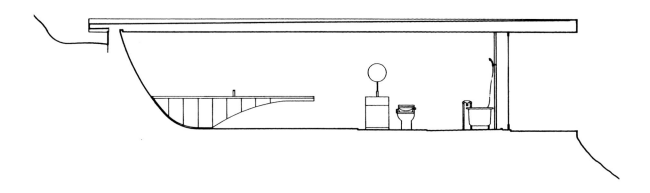

The section clearly reveals the architect's determination not to affect the land. Alterations are minimal, and the house rests on the site.

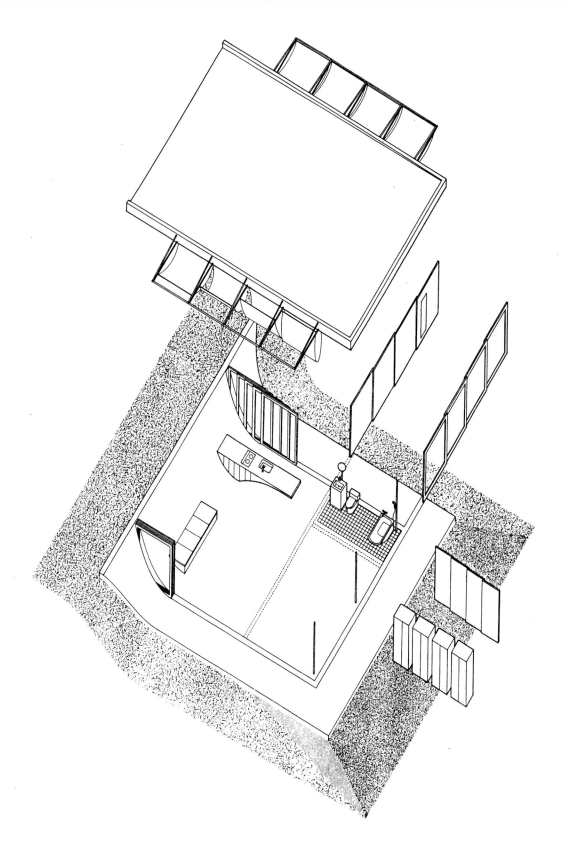

This house is an austere container of which its dimensions are based on the repetition of a module the size of a single bedroom. The front and side and side facades are clad in a serigraphed glass plate that forms a taut skin broken only by the rows of windows, the access porch, and by the garage door. This smooth surface functions as a huge screen that reflects the entire exterior during the day. In contrast, at night it reveals tiny episodes of the inner life of the house.

This box, cold and closed on the street side, opens onto the garden through a glass volume of exquisite purity. Large windows generate a direct relationship between interior and exterior. The rest of the facade is covered by horizontal wooden slats, arranged as a ventilated front. The material inside is birch wood, which provides a warm and pleasant atmosphere.

The refined construction and rigorous modulation together complete a minimalist project based on very few formulations that assumes a clearly objective role, characteristic of architecture far removed from the nature of the site.

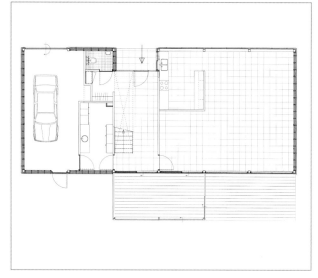

The structure is determined by the repetition of a module the size of a single bedroom. This compositional rhythm also provides the pattern for the windows.

The project was devised to endow the house with its essential character through a minimum number of elements.

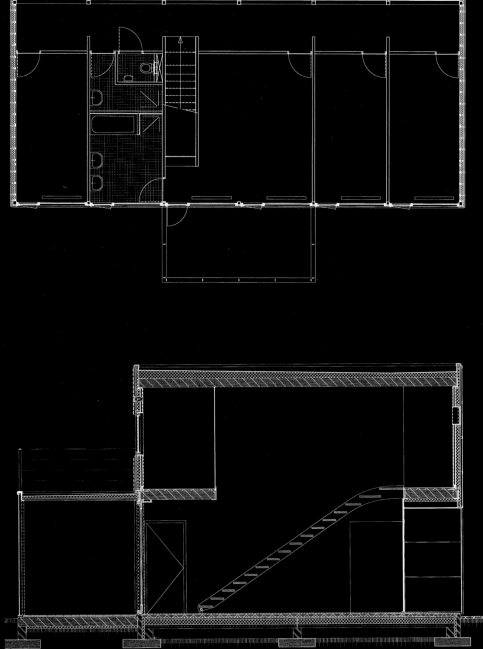

Conceived to be surrounded by gardens, this house stands beside a glen in Palmira, Cuernavaca. As yet unfinished, since a garden takes a long time to grow, the house is like a seed left to germinate in the earth.

This pavilion surrounded by greenery was conceived for functional reasons and as a compact whole that extends all over the site. Each room frames a different garden. The complex is based on four long walls and two concrete towers, and access is gained via a sloping plaza paved with local stone that passes beneath a shelter that will eventually be covered by bougainvillaea, and leads to the small vestibule. The living room is a deep terrace open to the northwest garden, surrounded by acacia and jasmine. The dining room is enclosed by long walls and adorned with abelia and nandina in an orange tree patio. The study shares a terrace with the swimming pool, while the bedrooms are submerged in a luxuriant garden.

In time the vegetation will gradually occupy the space designed for it. The mud walls, the concrete and the wood used for the planks will eventually age and become incorporated into the garden.

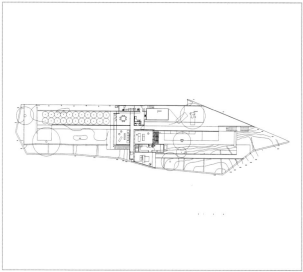

The house is conceived as a combination between interior and exterior spaces, designations blurred by the reflections and transparency of glass.

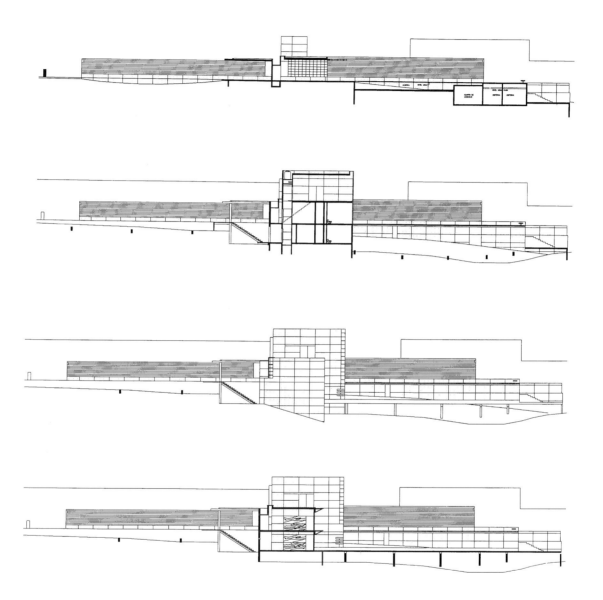

These sections clearly reveal the layout of the project: four long walls and two concrete towers. The arrangement of these elements determined the layout of the dwelling and the garden.

The concrete walls and the timber used for the planks will age as the plants grow and gradually occupy their place.

Apartment in Knokke
Claire Bataille & Paul Ibens

Knokke, Belgium

This medium-sized apartment is contained in a building with excellent sea views. The apartment is split into two levels, with different types of terraces at both ends.

The main idea was to group services (toilets, kitchen, cupboards, and so on) with the access elevator and interior stairs in the central zone. In this way, the need for vertical dividing elements was eliminated. At the same time, the interior space was maximized by the windows, providing light and views. This is particularly noticeable on the lower floor, where a pair of strategically placed sliding doors subdivide the space. On the floor above, the layout is the same, with the services in the central nucleus. However, since this is the bedroom area, the space is fragmented in order to provide greater privacy.

Especially significant is the new shape of the main floor's perimeter; small, secluded rest areas have been created around the windows to offset the presence of the sloping roof inside the dwelling and the many insets of the perimeter wall. These private rooms may also be closed behind their respective sliding doors.

The freestanding unit in the kitchen, consisting of the sink and storage, and the bathtubs in the bathrooms are both treated as objects of clear, clean forms. The use of dark stone endows their material presence with a hard and solid appearance.

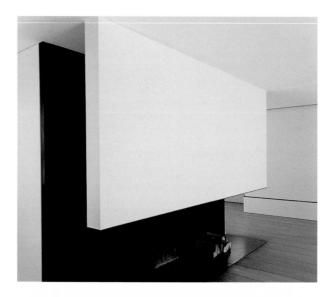

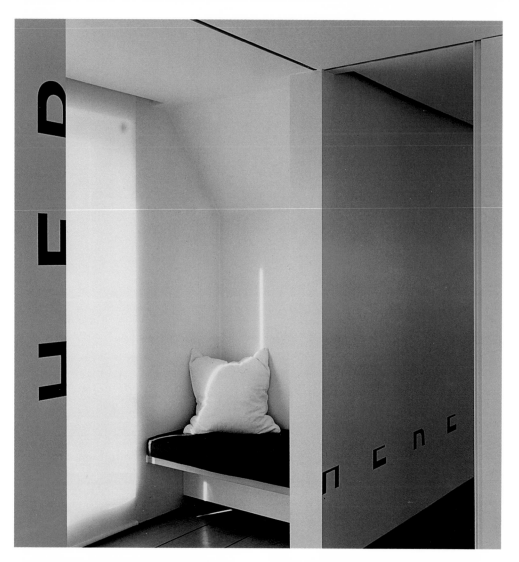

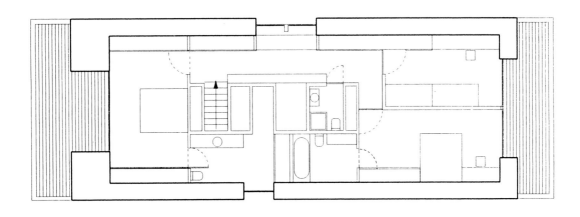

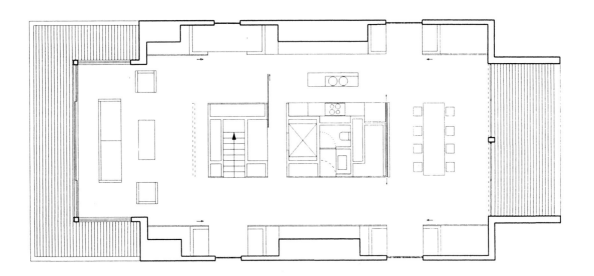

House in Viana do Castelo
João Alvaro Rocha

Photos © Luis Ferreira Alves, Hèléne Binet

Viana do Castelo, Portugal

Resting on a small contained square, this building is a simple, single-floor rectangular structure with a basement. The spare roof and side walls together define a rectangular framework which, like a large window looking toward the sea, contains the different rooms. Each room opens to the exterior through a system of wooden shutters that, when closed, align with the exterior cladding of the same material.

Although the house is encased in this simple framework, its interior spaces are complex, combining and contrasting with each other depending on the way the light strikes the different heights of the ceilings. Some elements, including the porch or the outer gate, are transparent, revealing what is on the other side. The spaces are arranged along the length of the framework, leaving the bathrooms further inside.

The use of color, the movable rear facade, and the subtle interplay between the ground, basement, and main platform levels endow this apparently rigid and totalitarian regular body with greater flexibility.

The window is a recurring symbol in this building, perhaps by virtue of the force of this work, born from the absolute simplicity of its architecture.

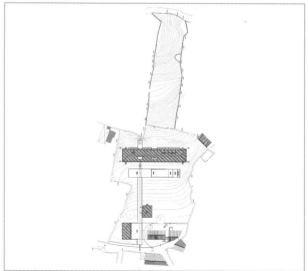

The interior is visually enhanced by the facade openings, which create multiple interplays of light.

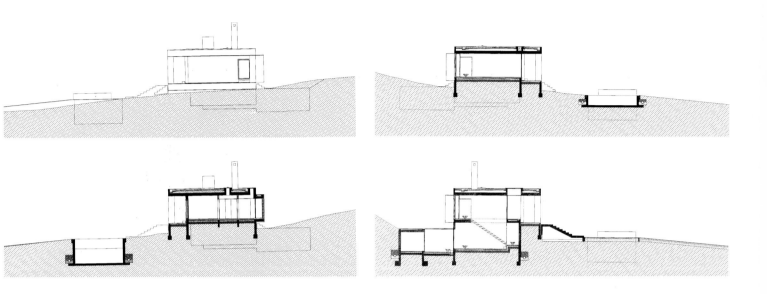

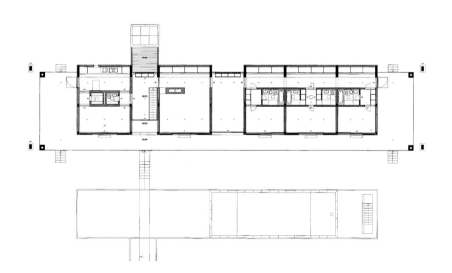

The finishes combine stone, wood flooring and partitions, and plastered walls and ceilings.

Private residence
Peter Marino

Photos © Peter Aaron/ESTO Photographics

New York, US

This 1,800-square-foot residence in New York enjoys 180 degree views over Central Park from the 77th floor of a tower clad in shining dark glass. The designer's goal was to create an elegant and peaceful minimalist interior that contrasts not only with the impressive views of the exterior but also with the owner's furniture and art collection. The interior space was designed using dressed French limestone, white Venetian stucco on the walls, and ebony. The interior ambience is completed with a set of designs in silver profiles.

All evidence of mechanical accessories has been eliminated. The columns conceal the air-conditioning. A single panel hidden behind a shiny wall coordinates all the control systems: temperature, lighting, security, audio/video, and communications.

A set of light oaken blinds opposite the top of the window is activated and lowered by remote control to reduce light penetration from outside. The original mullions of the window wall have been highlighted to obtain a grille of clear, precise profiles.

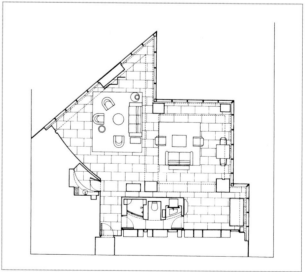

The project abounds in architectural devices that conceal the installations, such as the bathroom lighting, which is hidden behind the mirrors.

Apartment in Soho
Procter:Rihl

Photos © Hèléne Binet, Nathan Willock/View

London, UK

Built in the mid-1960s, the building that houses this apartment consists of simple apartments situated above unbecoming ground floor spaces containing offices and restaurants. The apartment originally consisted of a studio linked by a staircase to the bedroom and the terrace. The spaces were badly conceived due to the awkward positioning of the stairs and the excessive dimensions of the terrace in comparison to those of the apartment.

The interior space was extended upward and outward to provide views over the east and west ends of London. The layout of the apartment was inverted, placing the kitchen and living room on the floor above, while the bedroom, entrance, bathroom, and studio were relocated to the ground floor. The apartment was completely remodeled, including parts of the facade (the windows were replaced by sliding doors), and heat insulation was installed in the roof.

In general, the space was modified by simulating an increase in space through the strategic location of mirrors. Similarly, the definition of details contributed to creating the sensation of greater space. Frameless windows and light from above seem to prolong the walls, making them float outward. The definition of space has been achieved subtly through the use of contrasting materials, without the need to separate rooms, so many different materials have been used inside the apartment. Similarly, materials can also unite spaces, so the marble at the entrance is elongated toward the bathroom as if the two together formed a single unit.

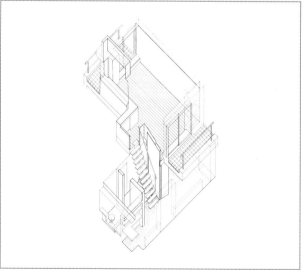

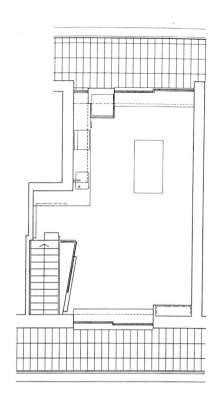

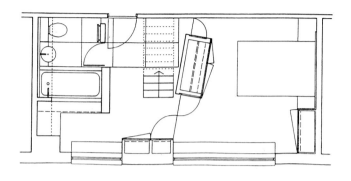

The custom-designed tables were conceived as delicate interior elements.

Montserrat/Quellos house
Josep Llobet

Photos © Josep Llobet

Girona, Spain

In its original state, the service areas (kitchen, pantry, washroom, and small bathroom) of this house, located on the edge of the old town center of Vidreres, in Girona, were very unorganized. Slight alterations to an extension of the ground floor and stairs to the floor above attempt to solve the problem of the inconveniences arising from the daily use of these services.

The renovation took the form of slight displacements of the walls, the creation of a large opening, and the addition of a skylight. These three elements were designed to impose order on both the service areas and the living spaces (living room, dining table area, and fireplace), all elements that are arranged around a central marble wall.

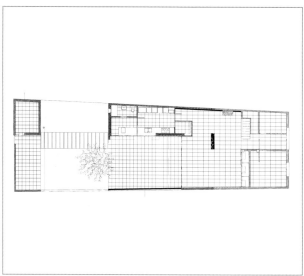

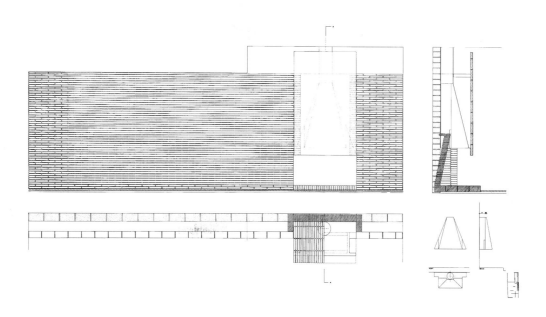

The kitchen, as well as the other service areas, combine functionalism and neutrality.

House in Ibiza
Stéphane Bourgeois

Photos © Pere Planells

Ibiza, Spain

This dwelling in the Balearic Islands is halfway between a traditional construction and a sophisticated contemporary house. The owner based his work on an old project and designed most of the elements that constitute the building. The distribution of rooms is based on a conventional plan: the ground floor accommodates the living areas and a guest room, while the master bedroom is on the upper floor. The visual division between the different spaces is via walls or the openings in them, changes in section that make it possible to subdivide the room to create different ambiances.

Special emphasis was placed on the surface finishes; the range of materials was reduced and a limited color range applied. The interior partitions are stuccoed and the floors are of continuous stone. There are no tiles, not even in the bathroom, where the floor, including the shower, is of polished pebbles. The project is coherent thanks, in part, to the furniture, which is almost entirely built-in.

The rustic furniture contrasts with the more refined forms, but creates no clashes in this varied, harmonious ambiance.

The living room is visually connected to the kitchen and the exterior spaces surrounding the house.

At first sight, the primary quality of the house seems to reside in its entirely monochromatic ambience. However, what is outstanding about the project is the ambiguity of its spaces in terms of location. The inner rooms are entirely permeable from the visual point of view: interrelated and open toward the exterior, they allow no introspection of any kind. Similarly, the patios are conceived as interiors: they are enclosed by walls that isolate them from the immediate landscape.

On the exterior, the dwelling incorporates elements of traditional architecture that protect it against the inclemency of the weather: thick walls provide thermal insulation, the walls are whitewashed to reflect the sun's rays, and openings are on the shady side, when possible. On the other hand, the interior—including the patios—has a contemporary, almost futuristic, air. The furniture combines white with a wide range of ochres, and includes exclusive, one-of-a-kind pieces. The kitchen opens onto the living room, which is characterized by pure lines, formal restraint, and the immaculate white of the smooth surfaces of the cupboards.

The interior is visually enhanced by the facade openings, which create multiple interplays of light.

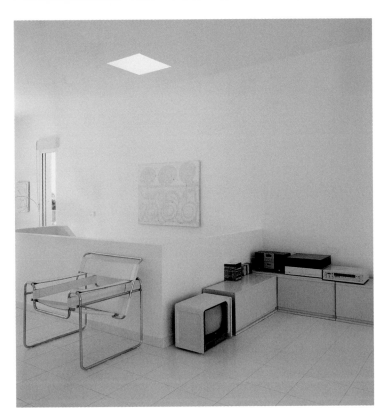

The M house
Kazuyo Sejima + Ryue Nishizawa

Photos © Shinkenchiku-Sha

Tokyo, Japan

This house stands in the center of Tokyo in a residential district of big houses. In general, the plots have a surface area of about 2,160 square feet. The facade overlooking the street is oriented toward the south, and for this reason many houses feature large windows on this side. The curtains are almost invariably drawn and high fences ensure privacy inside the homes. Given these circumstances, the architects decided to bring the exterior inside this home, while still ensuring the privacy of interior spaces.

The clients, a childless couple, required two studios, a guest room, two bathrooms, parking space for two cars, a bedroom for a future child, and a large salon in which to entertain.

The whole site was excavated, thus achieving greater vertical distance up to the street and adjacent buildings. Some rooms that required independence, such as the master bedroom, the guest room, and the garage, were placed at street level. The dining room, the study, and other open spaces were arranged on the floor below in combination with open patios. From here, street noise seems to come from far away, which further contributes to privacy inside the dwelling.

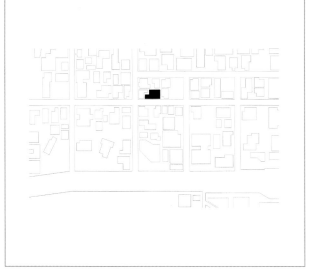

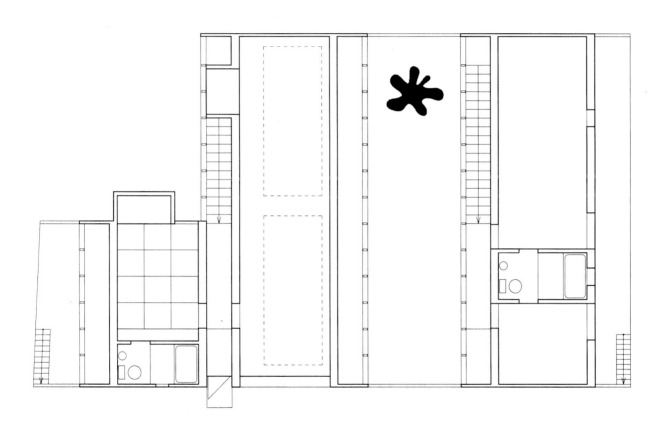

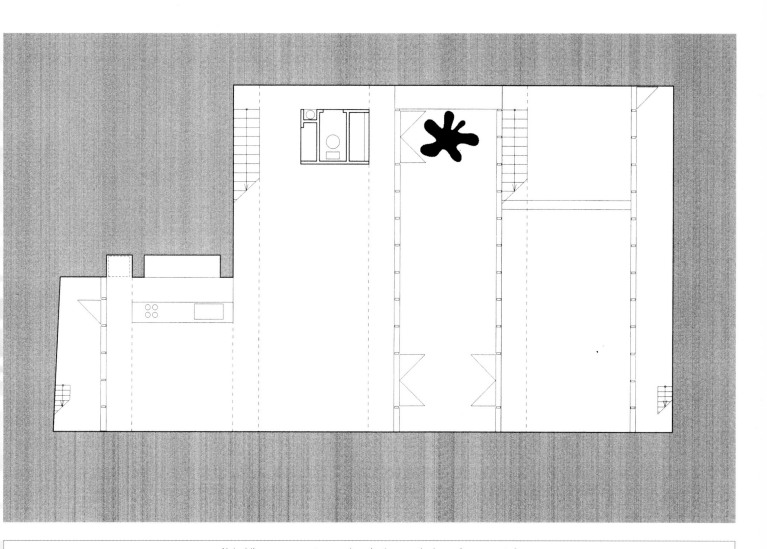

Naked lines are present everywhere in the way the house is represented.

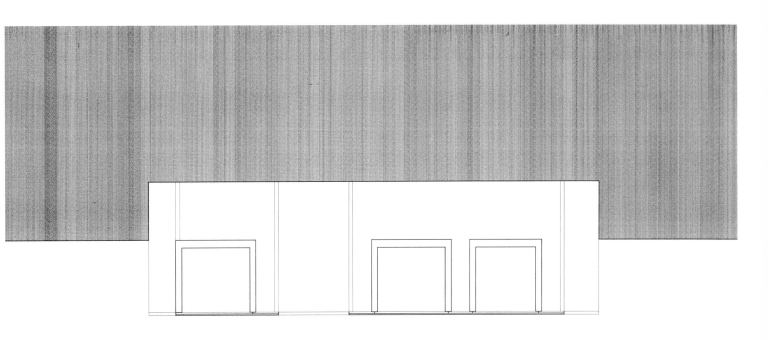

Resting on a small contained square, this building is a simple, single-floor rectangular structure with a basement. The spare roof and side walls together define a rectangular framework which, like a large window looking toward the sea, contains the different rooms. Each room opens to the exterior through a system of wooden shutters that, when closed, align with the exterior cladding of the same material.

Although the house is encased in this simple framework, its interior spaces are complex, combining and contrasting with each other depending on the way the light strikes the different heights of the ceilings. Some elements, including the porch or the outer gate, are transparent, revealing what is on the other side. The spaces are arranged along the length of the framework, leaving the bathrooms further inside.

The use of color, the movable rear facade, and the subtle interplay between the ground, basement, and main platform levels endow this apparently rigid and totalitarian regular body with greater flexibility.

The window is a recurring symbol in this building, perhaps by virtue of the force of this work, born from the absolute simplicity of its architecture.

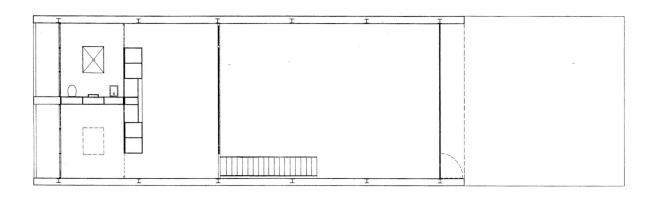

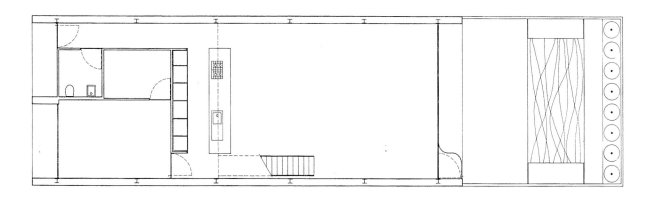

The kitchen is a single room beneath the mezzanine half-floor. The dining room and living room tables and the base of the bed and the towel-rail in the lavatory were all designed by the architects.

All the furniture had to be lightweight or mounted on casters so that it could easily be put aside to transform the house into a photographer's studio.

The treatment of the finishes and the light endow what is otherwise a very simple geometric space with a whole wealth of nuances.

This country house, which stands on a site in the urban center, was designed according to a minimal budget per square foot. From the outset, the main objective was to highlight the exceptional views of the La Vera valley, so it was decided that the main hollow should face west, where the sun sets behind the medieval castle on the hilltop less than a mile away. After an environmental study had been conducted on climate, site, and the program requirements, a design was developed with two concepts: a large common zone that articulates the whole project, and remaining pieces that serve and give meaning to the rest. The central area, 13.5 ft high, contains the passageways, common uses, main bearing walls, and, of course, the magnificent views.

The prominent east-west axis subsides when we enter the living area, which opens into a set of wider, lower rooms. In this way, the relationship between interior and exterior spaces is more flowing, and is accentuated by the natural light that comes from the perimeter zones. The exterior volume reflects the constructional system of bearing walls and concrete floor-to-ceiling structures.

The Huete house
Vicens/Ramos

Photos © Eugeni Pons

Madrid, Spain

To have at one's disposal a magnificent site, a generous budget, and solicitous clients is no guarantee that the project will be a success. While it is true that all these conditions facilitate the creative process, they may also become traps, causing the architect to be carried away by opulence, by superficial extravagance, and to give way to his most absurd caprices. Vicens and Ramos, however, have managed to avoid these snares; the result is a house of striking forms and exquisite finishes.

The common areas consist of large spaces divided by partial wooden walls that contain strategic openings that set up specific visual relationships. The finishes differentiate between the roles of the partition: the solid, stuccoed walls perform a structural function, while the timber partitions endow the ambience with warmth. The development of the section is very important in the upper parts of the house, allowing natural light to penetrate from above.

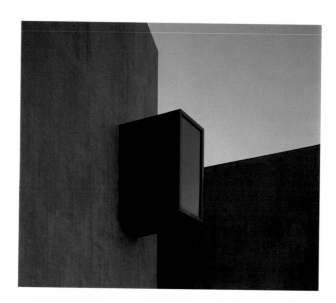

Like the rest of the project, the bathrooms are the result of clear, uncompromising decisions: purity of form and sections that endow each space with character.

3R house
Hiroyuki Arima

Fukuoka, Japan

This apartment is housed in a building that stands at a distance from the city center. Maples and cherry trees provide the landscape with colors that change as the seasons vary throughout the year. A small, twenty-year-old apartment block has been converted into a pleasant atmosphere in which to live. The exterior appearance of the building was left completely untouched, since any intervention of this kind was ruled out from the very outset. The building stands on a northward facing site that is flanked by a raised highway. Access to this restructured duplex is possible on the ground level via a set of stairs that connect with the road level.

The apartment is conceived as a continuous space, without fixed partitions. The name 3R alludes to three movable panels placed near the entrance of the apartment. By folding them at different angles, the space may be modified to provide a host of different combinations depending on the needs and tastes of each resident. The furniture was removed and the walls, floors, and ceilings were painted white to enhance the low intensity light that enters from the north. The rooms succeed each other on both floors, linked by a staircase. The original windows have been screened by translucent plastic panels, forming small spaces that may be used for storage, as a library area, or as a belvedere overlooking the garden.

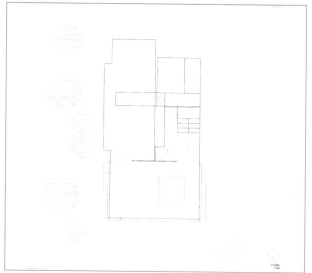

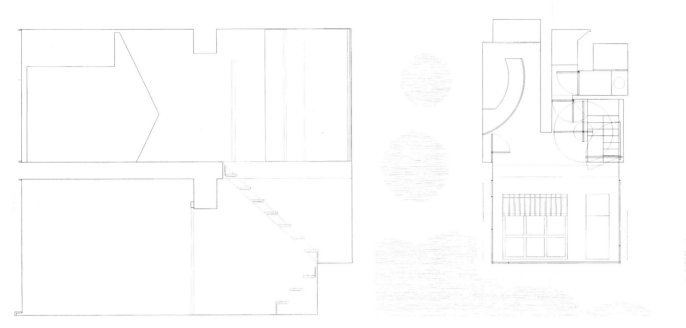

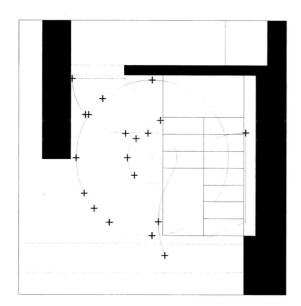
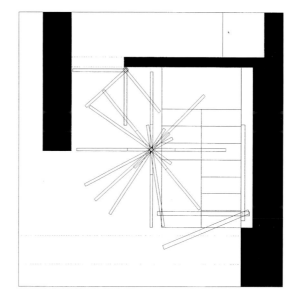

All projects by Hiroyuki Arima reflect characteristic Japanese sensitivity, a combination between tradition and futurism.